ATROCITIES AGAINST WOMEN AND YOUTH IN CONTEMPORARY SOCIETY

SHREYA CHATTERJEE

ISBN 979-888521097-3

Contents

Preface

This modern and advanced society as we are advancing in technology , lifestyles becomes easy and work becomes more swift and classified. This leads to several personal development in youth in their life, outlook , health and career front as well. But as the popular proverb entails "A coin has two sides", in the same way there are certain social perversions especially in the youth society of today which have become a major social problems in Indian society, to be further specific in approach several issues like alcoholism in teenagers, rates of pre-marital sex and live-in relationships is accelerates at a rapid pace, whereas marriage rates are declining and ratio of divorces to marriages are increasing and coming into the forefront. Does such issues only caters to criticisms or it adds on to several positivity to society as well? Why and how such issues be dealt with and what is the cause underlying such deviant activities of individuals in the society? Well, this work acts as a doorway to answer all of these questions that encompasses human life and the society around them.

As Brevity is the soul of wit. Accordingly, this present work is a modest attempt of the author to explain the inexplicable scenario of pervasive tendencies emerging in individuals in this modern era accompanied by several sociological research analysis and reports to give it an authentic essence for the betterment in understanding the society in which we live. This book reflects about all the atrocities faced by women and children and their impact on the society as a whole.

CHAPTER I

RISING RATIO OF WOMAN IN SOCIETY'S CRIME DIARY

Introduction-

Women are the most debated entity or issue in today's social world. We see the women of the society as an ornamental object of powers oppression for men. We always tend to have a sympathetic outlook for women, we consider her as a sexual object for men who is oppressed and subjected to bodily torture, harassments abduction, sadism in pornography and several sexual surgeries to enhance their sexual appeal in the eyes of men. In addition to this 'women if terminology refers not a mere female gender who is a sexual epitome for the whole patriarchal society but it also includes ideas like wife bettering dowry death, female child abortion, abduction etc. but somewhere we tend to avoid the other side of women which is challenging, filcre and has a great impact on human life in this century.

Women, rather is a not tool of oppression, she is a strong cup of coffee in a world that is drunk on the cheap wine of shallow esteem. Women are immensely involved in crime like weapon import and export, in field of black money earning, drug abuse cases and are having a ravaging effect in society harmony society's ethics as a whole and also in an individualistic sense as well.

Since creation of the American criminal system, the experiences of women either have not been sufficiently described or have been completely absent. **Gendered Justice** is a new term which we come across in the study of gender and crime. Sex differences in crime are differences between men and women as perpetrators or victims of crime. An observable difference between men and women might be due to social, cultural, unreported crime or biological factors like testosterone theories. Though crime statistics reported that men commit more criminal acts them women yet somewhere women are also in a cut-throat competition in regard to crime. Among the Indian states, according to the recent 'National Crime Record Bureau', the maximum no of women arrested under Indian Penal Code are from Maharashtra (28029) and then Tamil Nadu (21959). So, there is an increase in number of women coming in conflict with criminal law.

Key words: oppression, patriarchal society, women abduction, dowry-death, weapon import and export, drug abuse cases, black money.

Review of Literature

Carol Smart: According to this eminent writer, delinquent girls are likely to be of defective intelligence and more often than boys they are noticed to be 'over sized, bumpish, uncult and graceless..... According to Carol, women commit a range of offences including violent crimes that cannot easily be reconciled and criticized traditional theories of feminism as they failed to capture scope of female criminality.

Pat Cartlen: According to the book 'Criminal Women' Cartlen stated that contemporary theorizing in criminality should be based on an acknowledgement of social construction of Gender. She quotes 'Essential Criminal Women does not exist and other quotations like, 'Pules lost their' appeal as soon as I could legally cuter them.

Stacy L. Malliceat: According to his view, women and victimization prior to covering women as offenders because victimization if often a precursor to offending.

R. Perumal and Neethu Susan Cherian: They together published a book where they analysed a rise in crime committed by women between 2001-2011 is 5.4% to 6.2% and later it was observed the even it is 0.8% increase yet the nature and severity of crime has gone a drastic change. Now women are arrested for much harder and sophisticated crime.

Rani Dhavan Shankardass: This eminent personality highlight the fact that the prison voices from India are less crowded with women due to the so called belief that the female receives more punishment in communication than men.

Women increasing trend of criminality among juvenile girls

There is a violent increase in the rate of crime among teenage girls or juvenile girls. An examination of official police data in India has showed between that there is a vast increase in non-lethal violence committed by women rather girls since 1990s. in the TOI (Times of India) it was once reported that maximum number of women arrested under Indian Penal Code are from Maharashtra followed by Madhya Pradesh and Tamil Nadu most of them were between the age groups of 19-30 years. The reasons behind increase in crime by juvenile girls are neglectful and impartial treatment from parents, feeling of loneliness deprived of a good peer group and frustration.

Reason behind women involved in crime

Women involved in human trafficking/prostitution

Women are very often the offenders of women-hood. The women who supply other female victims for abduction or prostitution is due to several factors like Poverty, weak social and economic structures, lack of employment attraction towards a perceived higher standard of living.

Home, Office Report stated

- 8.9% men in London aged 16-44 years reported having paid sex in past 5 years.
- 75% of children abused through prostitution and went missing from schools.
- 85% women reported physical abused in family and45% among them reported familial sexual abuse as well.
- In U.K. 60% women involved in prostitution have been murdered in last ten years among 80000 women who work in on street prostitution. Average age of women involved in just 12 years old.

The ways to tackle the women who support this prostitution services are as follows:

Harm reduction involves the ongoing support of women and men who are involved and also supporting this sex services dealing with more short term issues such as safety, drug and substance use/ addiction, safer sex and HIV/AIDS prevention work. Work with women currently involved in prostitution needs to includes harm reduction as a necessary response for the once the factors behind women's involvement in prostitution are understood it makes no sense to label prostitution to do so would legitimize exploitation. Neither if we accept prostitution as exploitation, it is fair to criminalise those who are abused or exploitate ? in what other are of 'violence against women' would we criminalise the victims.

We do not view prostitution as a choice for women irrespective of age, and believe that it is contradictory to condom child prostitution while condoning or ignoring about prostitution.

Legislations for prostitution: For buying sex the first piece of Scottish legislation to tackle the purchase of sex was introduced in October 2007. This made it an offence to solicit in public places for the purpose of obtaining the services of prostitution. Prostitution public places Act 2007 (Scotland). Currently it is an offence to buy sex in Scotland.

The law to Sell Sex: Civil Government Act 1982 declared that women and men selling sex can be charged with soliciting under section 46 of the civil Government Act 1982. Start term but also should be working to end prostitution forever. Harm reduction must be coupled with intervention to support women leave prostitution, which can often take years. These interventions are needed to offer safe accommodation, drug treatment robust counseling and support services and learn new skills and training for future use. Some people believes especially researchers views that it is native or unrealistic to aim to end sex service. It is also referred to as the oldest profession, infact slavery is the oldest and sex service or prostitution stems from slavery.

Decriminalization it is another main cause to support sex selling and buying service of women in Indian society. It is important to decriminalize prostitution and all forms of prostitution may be included i.e. street sex workers, Kotha service or red light area sex worker and so on. In order to be effective, the decriminalization must all involve and accompanied by women involved in prostitution, How and Why ?

Prostitution is a major issue which service as an exploitative tool for women as well as it also involves certain women who being a female figure of society supports such business. Now we will enhance certain valid scenario of this societal issue of prostitution. The women's support project views prostitution, as part of the spectrums of men's violence against women and it committed to raising awareness of it root causes and harmful impacts, both on those directly involved and on our wider culture. Women become involved in prostitution for variety of reasons such as homelessness, child sexual abuse, mental ill health, trauma, previous sexual violence and drug and alcohol misuse, money pressure and poverty. These factors which severely effects women-hood and for a women into prostitution, should not be mistaken as the causes of prostitution itself which is the demo for men to buy sex, then prostitution would not work as a survival behaviour.

- Criminalization of third party profiting from prostitution services.
- Criminalization of buyers of sexual abuses
- Prevention work to reduce the demand of men to buy sex
- Pro-active services to help women get out of prostitution, increasing access, to safe, drug rehabilitation and to ongoing support.

Therefore, it is necessary to support the decriminalization of selling sex, extending current legislation of buying sex to all values and setting including brothels, saunas, lap dance clubs and massage parlour.

Sex Trafficking

Myanmar is source country for women and children subjected to sex trafficking, both in Myanmar and abroad. It is also increasingly a destination and transit country for foreign victims, including women and girls from India. Some Myanma women and children who migrate for work abroad particularly to Thailand and China, as well as other countries in Asia, the Middle East and the United States are subjected sex trafficking. Myanmar women are increasingly transported to China and subjected to sex trafficking ; Myanmar government officials are occasionally complicit in this form of trafficking, as well as in the facilitation of the smuggling and exploitation or Rohingya migrants.

Sex Services in Myanmar : Condomswere banned in 1993 lust today condoms and ticklers sold on the streets of yangan (Myanmar). The Military government is adamantly against rule that there should be a loss of prostitutes in China-town Virginity is highly priced in Myanmar-Burma. Burma is said to be a land of virgins and restful night.

Myanmar is major source of prostitutes (an estimate of 25000-30000) in Thailand, with the majority of women trafficked taken to Ranong bordering south Myanmar, and Mae Sai, at the eastern tip of Myanmar. Myanma sex workers also operate in Yunnan, China particularly the border town of Ruili. The majority of Burmese prostitutes in Thailand are from ethnic minorities. Sixty percent of Burmese prostitutes are under 18 years of age.

The United States Department of State office to Monitor and combat trafficking in persons ranks Myanmar as a Tier 3 country.

Triggers for drug use in women

Drug use is often triggered by emotional conditions, and women tend to experience more emotional extremes than man do. The key triggers for drug use in women are :

Loneliness: women need social and emotional connections with other people to feel happy and fulfilled in their lives. Being alone or worse, being in a crowd but feeling disconnected from everyone, is a sensation that can lead a women to use drugs or to relapse in addiction recovery.

Until recently, gender differences in substance abuse habits were not recognized. But thanks to modern science, we now know that :

- Women become addicted to drug after using smaller doses and for shorter periods of time than man.
- Women can be more sensitive to the effects of certain drug because of sex hormones.
- Women who use drugs experience different changes in their brains than man do.
- A women's menstrual cycle could affect her withdrawal symptoms and likelihood to relapse in addiction recovery.
- Women are more likely to experience anxiety or depression

- Women are more likely to die from over dose of certain drugs than men are.
- Women can experience more physical effects from drug use than men.

Since more attention is now being paid to women's health, we have a deeper understanding of addiction in women, how it is initiated, what effects it has and ultimately, how to help women overcome addiction.

Body image issues: Women often use drugs to attempt to change the way they look. If they feel they are too fit, stimulants offer the false promise of easy weight loss. There are also other drugs that can be used to build extra muscle mass. When these approaches to changing one's body image do not work, which is likely, alcohol and still other drugs can be seen as a way to soothe the emotional pain.

Hunger: Women tend to be more affected by public opinion than men, and they also diet more often. Instead of giving in to hunger by eating, many women use this condition as an occasion to chastise themselves for wanting to eat too much or choose the wrong foods. Some will turn to drugs to make the hungry feeling go away without consuming more calories.

Stress: Women tend to take on multiple projects at work and at home, leaving little or no energy for themselves. They are also likely to feel other people's emotions or worry about their problems. All of this adds up to a high level of daily stress, which is a big alcohol or drug use trigger.

Fatigue: All that stress makes women feel tired. Instead of resting, we often do not give ourselves permission to take a break. This is a moment when the urge to use drugs could become strong.

What this really means is that women have traditionally struggled to fit into a male-dominated society. Their feelings of angst, discomfort and alienation were met with medicinal solutions from healthcare providers, or at their own hands. The stress of being a women drove many to drink or use other substances to self-soothe.

This sounds like some very old-fashioned thinking, but it can be documented in the history of women's medicine. In the early 1900s, opium was the drug of choice. Women who complained of moodiness or other signs of mental anguish were prescribed syrups containing opium to calm their nerves.

HIV/AIDS in Myanmar

Burma has the second highest HIV prevalence rate in Asia, after Thailand. Sex workers are particularly at risk. The criminal nature of sex work in Burma or Myanmar as it is prohibited by the 1949 Suppression of Prostitution Act, also contributes to the ineffectiveness of reaching out to sex workers in Myanmar with regard to HIV/AIDS awareness and condom usage. In 2005 in Yungon, there were 100 brothels and up to 10000 sex workers, mostly of the Bamar ethnic group, with between 70-90 percent having a history sexually transmitted infections and less than 25 percent having been tested for HI. An anecdotal study at that time found that nearly half of sex workers in Yangon had HIV/AIDS.

Conclusion

Women crime rates have been a major problem related to the security health and moralization of this society. The fact that inspite of several crimes been acknowledged by news reports and statistic reports worldwide yet many researchers and other common people still undermines such crime committed by women and become gender-bias. The paper explores several crimes which are already committed by women of this society and also explained the causes behind it. There is need for strict implementation of laws against such crime and more awareness regarding such issues.

Suggestion

1. In order to root out women criminals, there is a severe need to stop women violence in society and exploitation women in anyway should be nipped in the bud. The reason being is that victimization often leads to offenders.
2. The law of the Indian Penal Code must criminalise the buying of sexual acts and would lead to death sentence especially for women who engage in buying sexual act business in order to eradicate human trafficking and prostitution.
3. Increase in literacy rates among women and parents should be friendly as well as give sufficient time to their girl child as neglect and loneliness is the main cause of getting deviant and commit crime more and more rich thirst of a high standard of living and lastly in some rare cases women specially the teanagers just for the sake of following a modern lifestyle get addicted to drugs and come in association with vulnerable species to such as extent that they get trapped themselves and cannot escape lifelong.
4. Government should make an ecosystem where orphans and women without family i.e. who lost their family in war accidents or in any other way should be kept together under one roof and women should be given a chance to become a motherly figure to all those orphans (girls/boys). It will make them feel that they can also be a mother and an important part in the upbringing and protection of these orphans which is a far better feeling than getting deviant and bent towards crime.
5. It is a very radical cure for all these women who are severely involved in any type of crime, and it can be cured through the techniques of **Hypnosis** and **brain wash** program which will direct their moral to think in a positive way and they will be a harmonious member of society.

CHAPTER II

PRE-MARITAL SEX : A RISING SCENARIO IN SOCIETY

Introductions- One Indian Psychologist told the Washington post, that Indian Tradition has moved back and forth, between eroticism and sexual repressiveness. Sex to a large period of time was not a topic that people talked openly about in India. Casual sex was very rare and is still considered taboo by Indian families even in the hippest of crowds. But now in this 21stcentury, Indian Society has changed its outlook, especially among the youth of today's generation 'Pre-married sex' has become a rising phenomenon and its increasing trend has been observed to a great extent. This study focuses on the pre-married sex in the life of youth and the causes and impact of it in the society as well as in individual's life.

'Sex' is a term which denotes the biological distinction between males and females in society. And pre-marital sex relationship refers to the sexual activity practiced by opposite sexes before their marriage. It tradition society it was considered a moral issue which was a taboo in many cultures and a sin by a number of religion. But now, as society advanced it has become an increasing trend in the society which focuses on the sexual extension and thrust for bodily pleasure and satisfactory of individuals. Hence, nowadays it has become a common concept in the life of man. Moreover, in the present scenario some Hindu temples have several sexually explicit images on their walls. Many Indian authors has contributed several epic works and studies on pre-marital sex such as pre-marital sex is not a sin by Acharya Ashish, India in Love a book on marriage and sexually in the 21stcentury by eminent author Ira Trivedi and lastly a master piece presented by Chetan Bhagat named 'One Indian Girl are evidences which highlights the rising scenario of pre-marital sex in India. More people today are sexually active before marriage.

It has been found that even in India, data from a sub nationally representative study of Indian youth conducted in 2006-2008 stated that out of 2408 married or un-married youth aged 15-24 had pre marital sex. This proves that pre-marital sex has become a very casual trend among the youths of India and the reasons behind it are truly practical and affects a lot on our perdition of system.

Reasons behind Pre-Marital Sex

1. **Available of Contraception**– In each and every medical stores of India, contraceptive pills and pregnancy detective kit have become a very common access. With this wider use of contraceptives young women or men do not fear unwanted pregnancy so much as earlier generations did. This took away most of the anxiety about unwanted pregnancy and also increased the level of curiosity of sexual pleasures before marriage in adolescents.
2. **Reduced parental supervision**– Teenagers are less supervised after school if both parents work full time and may take advantage of this opportunity for sexual activity. Increased facility of higher education means a lot of individuals (men or women) live for away from their families and hence, there is no social restriction and less has reduced parental supervision. This also indirect leads to meet the curiosity of sexual pleasures before marriage.
3. **Late marriage or declining marriage trend**– due to several education facilities and increased competition in employment in society, every individual wants to sore high in their career and due to the cut throat competition level in the job markets, individuals tend to struggle over a long period of time. Hence it results into late marriage or declining marriage trends. This indirectly serves as a reason behind pre-marital sex in Indian society in order to meet their sexual instincts.
4. **Gender equality in job**– in the earlier societies, women used to be more economically dependent on fathers or husbands. With

greater economic independence and increase in female headed households, women are free to control their sex lives. Therefore, more pre-marital sex and increased single parenthood exists in society

ADVANTAGES OF PRE-MARITAL SEX RELATIONSHIPS

Chemistry between the couple at the time of sexual intercourse is usually said to have increased. It not only creates an understanding between the two but also creates a good mutual respect between the couples. Still, it might be advisable only to have intercourse occasionally as making it a regular practice before marriage will surely lower your interest. Some people prefer to have intercourse within the same gender before marriage.

This is a denial scenario since it may make the person to lose interest of having the intimacy with the opposite gender. They will not have an experience or a feel of having intercourse with opposite gender and it automatically sets their mind to deny them even after their marriage. The ultimate advantage is you can clearly get to know each and every proceedings of bed step by step and you actually start to enjoy and co-operate with your partner which always makes you feel so excited and anticipated. You can clearly note your partner inch by inch physically and may be tempted to explore more and more about your partner. In this way it is very much helpful in noting down the actions and behavior of your partner which would prove handful even after the marriage. Some may have problems in fulfilling the desires of their partner while the other may get fulfilled very quickly. **To best avoid this problem, having intercourse before marriage will surely help you a lot. Once if you find either you or your partner is not able to fulfill each other , you can follow practicing some remedies to get fit enough and give the libido your partner wants.**

Disadvantages of having Sex before Marriage- Similar to the benefits, there are also some major disadvantages of having sexual intercourse before marriage. They are Based on the recent study, it has been revealed that man and women have lost their interest in having sexual intercourse with their partner after marriage as they have got fed up and tired of having intercourse with the same partner even before marriage. In some cases, there are also some males who have witnessed the same issues very frequently. Having intercourse before marriage may give them the attraction and physical fulfillment at the moment but it won't last long. The reason being that men always think that this just a part of relationship whereas the women think that they have given their entire life to the guy and become more close to him. In such cases when there is nothing more left in the relationship to be carried further, there are heavy chances of breaking-up, being a possibility. Also many women lose interest of having sexual intercourse after marriage with her partner just because of the myth that was created in her mind that intercourse will only lead to the fulfillment of individual on their own rather than the love and intimacy which is to be shared in the bed with each other. This is mainly because of her previous experiences at the time of her relationship. Whenever there is relationship between the men and the women before marriage which gets further through the sexual intercourse will get a feeling of individual's joy and pleasure on their own at the end of intercourse. The reason being the libido and the intimacy that was shown at the initial phases of first few weeks of intercourse will totally get changed into a entirely different one which has the desire to get fulfilled by the individual's on their and get their due disrespect and opinion towards the sexual intercourse even after the marriage. There are also several health related issues which may occur during premarital sexual intercourse. There may be problems during the period of life after marriage such as loss in erection, getting fulfilled quicker than usual and several other similar issues that are related to intercourse which occurs either before or after marriage affecting your future marriage life.

Premarital Sex and Religious Ethics - Sex is a notoriously difficult subject to study. There are all sorts of reasons people dissemble about what they do in the privacy of the bedroom, and you can imagine those incentives are even stronger when you're a woman in a conservative Muslim household being asked whether you had sex before marrying your husband. Aware of these challenges, the researchers ran several statistical tests to assess respondents' truthfulness. They found that Muslims and Hindus were actually the least likely of all religious groups to fib about premarital sex. This could suggest that Muslims and Hindus have fewer transgressions to lie about; or it could mean that Muslims and Hindus are better dissemblers, given the heightened consequences of premarital sex in those cultures. All major religions prohibit premarital sex, but Muslims appear to take Islam's proscriptions especially seriously. Why? Inorder to know whether the lower level of premarital sex among Muslims was driven more by individual choice or by the force of national culture. To test this, a survey looked at how the probability of a Muslim woman having had premarital sex changes depending on how dominant Islam is in the country where she lives. It has been found big effects: Muslim women living in countries with very few Muslims overall are more than three times as likely to have had premarital sex as Muslim women in countries where 90 percent of the population adheres to Islam. While the researchers offer explanations for Muslim chastity, they have less to say about why Buddhists rank highest in premarital sex. They offer that it could be because Buddhism is not monotheistic and has fewer "strict rules about specific behaviors." of course Hinduism is not monotheistic, either, and, indeed, the field study done for the study reflects on whether some religions effectively promote the search for pleasure. Christianity according to Bible donot approve of sex before marriage because the believe that it would be non ethical but at the same time they forgive premarital sex done as they believe once an individuals confronts god he becomes a new creation of God.

Premarital Sex – An Increasing Trend Among Teenagers -Teenagers who feel incomplete, inadequate and unappreciated are more likely to seek comfort in a sexual relationship. But those with a life rich in relationships, family traditions, activities, interests and — most of all — consistent love and affirmation are less likely to embark on a desperate search for fulfillment that could lead to unwise sexual decisions. Those who have a healthy, productive faith in God are more likely to have deeply 145 Journal of Current Science (January, 2019) rooted reasons to respect and preserve the gift of sex and to respect rather than exploit others.

Be aware of these specific risk factors for teen sex:

Alcohol and drug use: Aside from reflecting problem attitudes (rebellion, poor selfconcept, invulnerability) that make sex more likely, intoxication also clouds judgment and weakens resistance to sexual overtures. A steady boyfriend or girlfriend: Strong attachments and feelings of exclusivity invite nature to take its course, especially when physical expressions of affection begin early in the relationship. This is a particular risk in a situation where the boy is more than two or three years older than the girl is. If a teen romance appears to be getting hot and heavy and a lot of physical contact is already displayed, you will need to speak with both boy and girl diplomatically but candidly about the physical process they are setting in motion.

Little parental monitoring: Leaving adolescents alone for hours at a time or not requiring accountability is a setup for sex.

A parental belief thatadolescent sex is appropriate: If you think premarital sex is okay, your adolescent will too and will act on that belief. A history of physical or sexual abuse: These acts against children and adolescents violate their bodies, minds and hearts. Sexual abuse creates a grossly distorted view of sexual behavior, destroys boundaries, and drives a deep sense of worthlessness into the emotions. Whether the abuse occurred in the distant or recent past, adolescents with this history need ongoing support, counseling and prayer to help them develop healthy attitudes about sex and about themselves.

Frequent family relocations: Moving generally stresses both parents and adolescents (especially if the kids resent the decision). This can erode parental authority and distract parents from involvement with their children. Bonds to social supports such as church groups that help prevent sexual activity are severed by multiple moves. Loneliness and loss of friendships may lead some teenagers to use sexual activity to gain social acceptance. These issues should be considered by parents who are thinking about a possible relocation.

Only one parent in the household: Parenting was meant to be a team effort, and some risks will naturally increase when one parent is left to do all the protecting and monitoring alone. Some studies do indicate that adolescents living with a single parent are more likely to become sexually active than those living with both parents. Work and household demands can prevent single parents from being as involved and attentive as they need and want to be. And the divorce and desertion that sometimes lead to a one-parent home can make teens uncertain about the value of marriage as the setting for sexual activity and about the role of sexuality in parental relationships. This increased risk does not mean that adolescent sex is inevitable in single-parent families. But it does place an additional responsibility on single parents to send their teenagers clear and consistent messages about sexuality. And it is one more reason for single parents to enlist as much support as they can.

Other Factors Influencing Premarital Sex Among Adolescents–

- Trend of Casual sex among peer groups just for the sake of curiosity about sexuality.
- Trend of increasing alcoholism among teenagers leads to increase in sexual urges unconsciously.
- Trend of friends with benefit category which is a typical relation based on sexual intercourse devoid of any emotional knots.

- The competitive socio economic life leads to more complexity in job opportunities leading to stress and frustrations which can be very effectively relieved by indulging in sex.

Therefore it can be concluded that premarital sex has been highly prevalent in a country like India which is considered to be a developing country till date. Sex is no more taken as a taboo and it is rightly believed that Sex is a human need, and in addition to it there are several factors which influences sexism in a very casual sense. Parental members should not feel hesitated to discuss about contraceptives, pregnancy, abortion and other terms related to premarital sex life so that children in their future life feels free to share their problems and deal every situation wisely without judging themselves through the eyes of society. On the other hand, society should not humiliate and hold on to conservative thoughts filled with negativity regarding pre marital sex, rather society should treat it casually as it is a act of reciprocity not an individual imposition. But at the same time as it is said that a coin has two sides, it is always necessary for the adolescents to be aware of premarital sexual relations and take every step wisely and in a calculative manner so that problems such as pregnancy or abortion or high consumption of contraceptives do not lead to negative impact on health. However inspite of being calculative awkward situations may arise which should be handled with care.

Conclusion– this study directs towards a positive approach towards pre marital sex in Indian society and strengthens the feminism belief in India. Pre marital sex has been raising to such an extent those same Indian cities it is no more considered to be a taboo. For example, in the city of Bangalore, the individuals prefer more live in relationship than any other Indian city. The average age of person loosing virginity is 22 again cities like Delhi, which is the capital of India claims to be the most open minded and extending trends of modernization and variant sex education has become the major reasons to support pre-marital sex. So it can be concluded that even in India, conservative thinking has been abolished to a large extent, they too believe that it is never wrong to live our life in our own way with an essence of pre-marital sex which is a pretty casual phenomenon now.

Suggestion

1. First and foremost individuals themselves should adopt a feminist approach towards life, ones outlook should be brand and open minded so that individuals must not consider pre-marital sex as profane and should not consider pre marital sex as a symbol of impurity in aspects of marriage. A healthy marriage is based on love and understanding and not on the basis of virginity.
2. Secondly, sex education with pre-marital highlight should be introduced as a subject in school so that an individual from grass-root level becomes aware of its positive impact in individual's life and society. And gradually if wide become a casual phenomenon in one life.
3. A respect towards ones personal life must exist. An individual has full right to live his life in their own principle, supporting the phenomenon of pre-marital sex or avoiding pre marital sex is his own will. Society cannot impose a universal rule to be a negative concept for everyone.
4. Strict implementation of loves should be made a make pre marital sex legalized. After all a pre marital sex and a live in relationship can lead to better bonding and understanding in ones marriage life.

CHAPTER III

SOCIOLOGICAL STUDY ON THE PRE-MARITAL SEX AND LIVE-IN RELATIONSHIP AMONG YOUTH :

Background of the study- The pre-marital sex and live-in relationship among the young people rather teenagers or youth nowadays are increasing at an alarming rate. Remote consequences of such high risk behavior are increase in the incidence of STDs including HIV, unsafe motherhood, single mother child or abandoned child, juvenile delinquency and many more.

The major objectives of the study – The significant objective of study are as follows,

- To investigate about the high- risk of sexual behaviors in depth.
- To study factors influencing such behaviors like age at sexual debut, type of partners , consistent condom usages, hostel stay, and socio economic profile of college going youths specially male ones.

Materials and methods to study the research problem- The study was conducted in Jamnagar among undergraduates(18-24years)male college students. A total of 450 students were randomly selected from three colleges of Jamnagar. Observant as well as Questionnaire methods are adopted to get appropriate results.

Resultant of the study - Out of 450 students taken for analysis,

- 49.11% were in age group of 18-20 years.
- Among study subjects, 13.78% had one or more pre-marital sex relationship exposure.

- In students with positive sex history , 95.16% were girlfriends, 14.5% were commercial sex workers, homosexuals were 6.45% and multiple sex partners were 33.88% .
- Among students, 62.9% were using condoms continuously and consistently.
- Three-fifth of the ones indulged in the pre-marital sex were in the age group 16-20 at the time of sexual debut.

Conclusion of the study- Most of the students were very young at the age of pre-marital sex exposures. Consistent condom usage was not uniform. The students staying at hostels, indulged in pre-marital sex, were found to be have multiple sex partners.

(A STUDY BY RESEARCHER SUDHA B YADAV, M.P SHAH MEDICAL COLLEGE, JAMNAGAR, GUJRAT)

CHAPTER IV

STRUGGLE TO BLEND ORTHODOXY WITH MODERNITY: GENDER AND SEXUALITY, CHALLENGES AND RESPONSES

A Thin line between Sex and Repressions:

At first sight, the topic might seem to be weird for this modern century where pre-marital sex and living relationships are raging at an alarming rate, and every man and woman in India are living their wet dreams. Quite contrary to the anticipation, until today, sexuality in Indian society has remained with a hidden pathology of desperateness inside folks. The situations are like hearts are raging volcano of sexual frustrations and Playboy magazines and patriarchal pornography provide nothing to quench the thirst that they possess in their mind and soul rather underneath their undergarments. India is still a country where men don't have enough women for themselves and living a life of ultimate drought. Parents still feel hesitant to open up and have a word with their children about sexuality, which makes children more curious about it and gradually their involvements in unprotected sex rise with serious consequences .Some of our learned intellectuals in their books state that India is Independent it's a free India and sex is a basic human need. Sexuality is not only confined to the walls of intercourse, but it has a profound effect on society's other realm as well. Indian politicians are vocal in extending malice towards the people who freely express themselves or refuse to be dictated about their clothes and lifestyle. But why, if our constitution has provided us with all sorts of fundamental rights of speech and right to freedom, then **why even reaching this modern century we cannot express our personal views openly without dispute?** Till date it has been acknowledged that every year on 14thFebruary which signifies Valentine's day, the day of lovers, the couples are beaten up by the police if they are expressing love in public, closing of night clubs and bars and chastising women who dress-up as indecent are on the peak!

These repression is having a serious impact on the crime diary of India. Urges towards knowing the unknown is increasing, increasing rates of sexual crimes are taking place gradually in the nation. India currently occupies the third largest position of HIV infected population, among which more than 85% are having unprotected sex. The underlying cause behind the fact that our daily newspapers are full of inhuman stories of rape cases of minors is 'the thin line between sexuality and repression. There was an inexplicably beautiful movie named **'Masan'**which had a famous dialogue **that compared life to a Condom**. I think life cannot have such accurate definition to itself in any of the writings of great authors which explains that life is a temporary affair that lasts only in pursuit of that one moment of overwhelming happiness. Yet, it's very sad that being the crowd of this century keeps being dutiful towards false morality and tend to ignore sex as a basic emotional, psychological and physical need of the society.

On the one hand,stretching list of Gangrapes across the nation has enraged people immensely. Previously, in 2012,when **Nirbhaya**was brutally gang-raped in a moving bus in Delhi which shook many people's conscience is unfortunately not a fullstop punctuated in the society. The sad part is nothing has changed after so many promises and right after we acknowledge the **Kathua girl**case who was just eight years old, Manipur girl was raped and set on fire at the age of 11, and the list goes on and on. But on the other side of the mirror we see an orthodox society preaching morality and ethics that represses sex and its practices, where girls are made conscious about their attire and their exposure just because of the fear of getting sexually exploited, where women masturbation, orgasm, and talk about sex in a way often restricted. This contradictory scenario of the society has a simple answer to it-

"repression increases the urge of knowing the cause behind being repressed". Hence, it is very important to liberate sex in every corner of India and is a very sensitive issue to be pondered upon with deep understanding.

IMPACT ON INDIVIDUALS DUE TO STEREOTYPE ORTHODOXY REGARDING GENDER AND SEXUALITY:

" Adultery causes earthquakes? Sexual repression can cause much worse." Firstly, Nothing inspires murderous mayhem in human being more reliably than sexual repression. Denied food, water or freedom of movement, people will get desperate and some may lash out at what they perceive as the source of their problems. But if expressions of sexuality is thwarted, the human psyche tends to grow twisted into grotesque, enraged into perversions of desires. Unfortunately the distorted rage resulting from sexual repression rarely takes the form of rebellions against people who are behind repressions but exceptions of course exists everywhere in this society. The rage is generally directed at helpless victims who are sacrificed to gods of guilt, shame and ignorant pride. Secondly, Gay and conservative author Andrew Sullivan has written in one of his work that "the suppressions of these core emotions and the denial of their resolution in love always leads to personal distortion and compulsion and loss of perspective. Thirdly and Lastly, following a famous sociological theory of logical and non logical actions by Vilfredo Pareto, it is righteously stated that individuals tend to get inclined more towards non logical actions which are motivated by emotions than logical actions which are motivated by reasons, therefore restricting sexual activities can lead to increase in the urge of knowing in men , and if yet it is suppressed may lead to rape attempts on anyone who is well acquainted and in close proximity with that person. Our daily newspapers depicting cases of underage children and babies facing sexual torture is a major evidence to it. Hence, It is always healthy to be free and open about sexuality and concepts related to it.

IMPACT ON SOCIETY DUE TO STEREOTYPE ORTHODOXY REGARDING GENDER AND SEXUALITY:

Firstly, suppression of sexual activities or its related information can never be healthy for anyone's health. Suppressing desires creates pressure on sexual hormones as well as physical health and disorders leading to several severe side effects and even brain perverseness which in turn has a serious social consequences in the form of social violence.

Secondly, Repression of sex related information in society not only effects the health of individuals but also effects the health of society as it builts up frustration of not being able to meet his sexual desires and express freely which leads to increase in rape cases, stereotype mentality of forcefully indulging in it , domestic violence etcetera.

Lastly, repression leads to Honor killing , which refers to the homicide of a member of a social group due to the perpretrator's belief that the victim has brought shame and disgrace to the society or community usually for reasons such as refusing to enter marriage, having sex outside marriage, dressing in sense which are deemed forbidden or engaging in homosexual relations. Hence, such stereotype mentality create a strong impact in the societal eyes for those people who are indulged in sex and in turn kills the 'honor' of that individual accompanied by several social consequences.

Female Sexuality: An Intertextual Analysis of Rabindranath Tagore and Satyajit Ray:

1. As we approach the one hundred and fiftieth birth anniversary of Rabindranath Tagore, it is necessary to re-define and reiterate the far-sightedness and comprehensiveness of his work on our own terms. If the Nobel Prize carried his words beyond Indian shores as early as the second decade of the twentieth century, the cinema as a visual medium popularised in the later decades, was instrumental to a large extent in exposing him at various international forums. In this essay, I will attempt an exposition through the meeting point of the two men—India's first Nobel laureate Rabindranath Tagore and her only life-time Oscar winner, Satyajit Ray. Andrew Robinson, writing of the link between the two says, 'Tagore and Ray are indissolubly bound. If non-Bengalis know Tagore at all today, it is mainly by virtue of Ray's interpretations of him on film.
2. The question to be raised in this essay is how do these two geniuses Tagore and Ray, complement (or confront?) each other in the exploration of the status of women in the upper class society of Bengal? The changing status of women, a product of the social reform movements of the nineteenth century, must be viewed against the emergence of the monotheistic Brahmo Samaj, its protest against Hindu polytheism, orthodoxy and the concomitant social evils like the caste system, the victimisation of women in a patriarchy through the practices of

sati (immolation of a widow on the husband's funeral pyre), child marriage and *kulin* polygyny.

3. I have deliberately posed the question of confrontation because the intertextuality of fiction and film, of translating the written word onto the cinema screen, is at best problematic. Robert Stam, in an introductory essay on *The Theory and Practice of Adaptation,* says, 'The conventional language of adaptation criticism has often been profoundly moralistic, rich in terms that imply that cinema has somehow done a disservice to literature.Stam goes on to say that one of the sources of hostility to adaptation is iconophobia, the fear of exposing the subtle symbolism of the written word to the more explicit iconography employed by the cinematographer. While this essay will delve into the possible ramifications of this fear in the context of the two, its primary connotation emerges in the cinema's handling of the works of a literary figure who is Bengal's most revered icon, who, even today enjoys bardic status, even when the maker of that adaptation is no less a figure than Satyajit Ray. It is further problematic because the subject under consideration here is Tagore's analysis of the emergence of the New Woman (*nabeena*), battling the confines of prescribed space within the *andar mahal/antahpur* (inner domain) of the home in a patriarchal society in a pre-colonial context. How does Ray, paying his centennial tribute to Tagore in the 1960's and thereafter, present this to a more permissive post-colonial generation for whom the stained glass windows of the *andar mahal* of Victorian mansions had long since collapsed. Talking of just such a dilemma of depicting Charulata's barely-controlled extra-marital passion for her brother-in-law Amal in Tagore's short story *Nastanirh,* on which Ray made a film he called *Charulata,* Andrew Robinson comments, 'Like so much that Tagore did, Nastanirh attracted adverse criticism from Bengalis at the time. The story gave the foundations of family life a shake, which many people resented. He (Ray) found people still sensitive to the issue sixty years later, 'A lot of people seemed

to think it was a very risky subject because of the illicit relationship. I never had any such doubts at all. I made the film and it was proved that I was right, because it was very widely accepted.The contentious issue of repressed sexuality of the new woman vis à vis the old, will be examined in this essay with particular reference to two of Tagore's works, his novel, *Ghare Baire* (The Home and the World) and his short story *Nastanirh* (The Destroyed Nest) both of which were made into powerful movies by Ray.

4. Any discussion on the changing status of women must be viewed as earlier noted in this essay, against the socio-religious background of the Brahmo Samaj and the resultant reform movement of the Bengal Renaissance. With the spread of Western education and the availability of Western texts, the bi-lingual upper-class élite in Bengali society was deeply influenced by Western philosophy and the histories of social revolution and religious reform in Europe. Raja Rammohan Roy (credited with being instrumental in the abolition of *sati*) and Dwarkanath Tagore (Tagore's grandfather), established the monotheistic Brahmo Samaj.The Samaj was at the forefront of the social reform movements of the time. It was more egalitarian in worship than the Hindu religious order, allowed free mixing of the sexes in the prayer meetings, called for female education, widow re-marriage and the advancement of the age of marriage for girls. It benefitted not only the members of the Samaj, but brought about the winds of change through the Bengal Renaissance of which humanists like Tagore, the novelist Bankim Chandra Chatterjee,educationist Iswar Chandra Vidyasagar and the religious leader Swami Vivekananda, were at the forefront. Incidentally, Satyajit Ray was also a member of the Samaj. However, this socio-religious movement of the Samaj, also caused a deep divide within Bengali society between those committed to reform and those entrenched in Hindu orthodoxy—a divide nowhere more evident than in the plight of the occupants of the *andar mahal* and that of their more

liberated counterparts. Partha Chatterjee calls it the spiritual/ material dichotomy.

5. The *andar mahal* was a sacrosanct domain within which upper class women were contained and confined by a patriarchal society, unseen by men beyond the immediate family and to which even husbands had access only at night. The nineteenth century re-invented this domain as a sort of sanctum sanctorum of Indian spirituality and heritage in what Partha Chatterjee calls the last frontier of uncolonised space where no encroachments by the coloniser could be permitted by Indian men who were themselves exposed to Western culture and education and adhering to the Western value system in public life. The victim of this male desire for preservation of tradition was the woman, stereotyped as chaste wife (*pativrata stree*), willing womb or repressed widow. The ideals of womanhood in orthodox Hindu society were re-enforced by allusions to mythical and epical references to female chastity, thus introducing a religious dimension to the worship (Tagore uses the word *bhakti* at the beginning of *Ghare Baire*) and care of the husband. The emergence of the New Woman towards the end of the nineteenth century, educated, liberated, dressed differently from her more traditional counterparts and exposed to the 'provocations' of 'literacy and literature', yet confined to the *andar mahal*, precipitated a serious clash of personalities. It is this clash that Tagore exteriorises through the study of repressed female sexuality and Ray through a series of symbols signifying the dramatic turmoil within women like Charu in *Charulata* and Bimola in *Ghare Baire*. These are portraits of lonely, sensitive, dissatisfied women locked away in ornate affluence in enormous Victorian mansions. These women are counterpoised in both Tagore and Ray against their more traditional counterparts (*pracheena*). Instances of the latter are seen in Manda (Charu's brother's wife, and one of a large retinue of dependants thriving on her husband's largesse) and Bimola's widowed sister-in-law, also dependant on the generosity of

Nikhilesh, Bimola's *zamindar* husband in *Ghare Baire*. Bankim Chandra Chatterjee, in a serious critique of the dichotomy between the progressive woman and the orthodox in his essay *Pracheena and Nabeena*, decries the loss of a traditional value system, which included chastity, respect for and care of the husband, disciplined domestic labour and philanthropy as a religious observance. The *nabeena* he says, with her insufficient learning, has lost the values and the *dharma* of her traditional counterpart and not benefited from the values to be inculcated from modern education. Laziness and excessive leisure is at the root of all domestic ills.

Both Charu and Bimola fail the first requirement of patriarchal stereotyping, they are empty-wombed. Though they do not suffer the social stigma attached to the same owing to pride of position, their childlessness certainly generates the sexual crisis which later brings about their downfall and which motherhood might well have averted. The question whether they remain childless due to their husbands' treatment of them as if they are fragile commodities to be handled with care and reverence, remains unanswered. Their husbands are kind, gentle, affectionate and without any addiction to the typical upper-class vices of wine and women. Women like Charu and Bimola (as also Monimalika in Tagore's *Monihara*, filmed by Ray as part of his trilogy on Tagore's women characters), apparently have everything; large Victorian mansions scattered with expensive European bric-a-brac, (among them gilded, ornamental mirrors, whose significance will be discussed later in the essay) a retinue of servants, leisure, privacy and encouragement to pursue their literary hobbies far from the prying eyes of the large number of dependants who were an inevitable part of such households. These were privileges unknown to many of their less fortunate peers.

In *Monihara*, the husband showers jewellery sets upon his avaricious wife Monimalika (the name literally means a string of gems) in an effort to buy her love. Ironically the same jewels lead to her death, when she elopes with her cousin dressed from head to foot in her jewellery, in an effort to safeguard them from the husband she has never loved and grossly misunderstood. Both Nikhilesh and Bhupati are seen as Renaissance men who have inculcated reformist values with varying degrees of success. But while Tagore's novella *Nastanirh*, was written as a critique of men who called themselves reformers but were unsuccessful in implementing those reforms within their own homes, Nikhilesh in *Ghare Baire*, conducts a daring social experiment of exposing his wife before his friend and pays the penalty.The ideal of a more progressive marriage based on companionship which challenged female stereotyping, made impossible demands on these women in transition as Nikhilesh ultimately realises, 'In moulding the *sahadharmini* (a wife who shares her husband's vision), we corrupt the wife.

6. Yet these women continue to be dissatisfied and unfulfilled. Their peers who still remained confined within the category of the *pracheena* might have been overwhelmed with such bounty and devoted themselves to their service-unto-death vow to their lord and master. The attitude of willing self sacrifice which the *pativrata* traditionally practiced is described both by Bankim Chandra Chatterjee in his essay and Tagore at the beginning of *Ghare Baire*, as leading to a submergence of the ego, which was its own spiritual reward. In the novel, which follows the structure of a diary, Bimola in an introspective flashback, talks of the dangers of negotiating the chasm between the *pracheena* and the *nabeena*. She is initially eager to practice the rituals of service demanded of a *pativrata*, much to the distress of her educated husband who prides himself on his liberated views. She is unable to handle the freedom of choice her husband so generously grants her. At the end of the novel, Bimola returns to the *bhakti* and worship which is part of the *dharma* of the *pativrata*, but at this point she has to earn the right to offer that

worship which she has lost in the intervening period. Tagore's novel focuses on both these aspects of her character because it begins with a flashback. The scene of the changing of jackets before the mirror is a prelude to that. The reconciliation with her husband at the end in the film is executed through a passionate kiss rather than any offer of *bhakti*. Charu on the other hand, remains unaware of the growing demands of her blossoming body and the consequent restlessness as she flits bored and impatient from one inane task to the other, with time hanging heavy on her hands and no one to make demands on her. With the *nabeena's* periphery still in transition, these generous, considerate husbands, by not being 'demanding,' left unsatisfied the feminine desire 'to give' in a marital relationship. This desire was rooted in the traditional 'dharma' of womanhood with near-religious fervour. Tagore, analysing this chasm between the old and the new, says in *Monihara*, 'Traditionally, women like raw (sour) mangoes, hot chillies and stern husbands.The implication is that if a man does not make demands on his wife, he is considered to be weak, lacking in masculinity and does not command respect from his wife.

7. Into such a scenario enters the third of the love triangle. The arrival of Charu's young brother-in-law (is heralded by a storm in Ray's film, in which shutters bang, the birdcage swings violently and the room is in turmoil. In the film *Ghare Baire*, the demagogue Sandip arrives on the shoulders of his saffron-clad followers with shouts of '*Vande Mataram*' rending the air against the background of the *swadeshi* movement triggered off by Lord Curzon's attempts to partition Bengal in 1905–06. Bimola watches along with other womenfolk from behind the purdah of a bamboo curtain and at one point, mesmerised by his rousing speech, she unconsciously parts the curtain and their eyes meet. Bimola's diary records her introspective comments in the novel: 'Was I the bride of the palace? At that moment I was the sole representative of Bengal's womanhood—and he, the manhood/ icon of the bravery of Bengal.The enhancement of her own

image to identify with the Motherland/Mother Goddess concept is part of her growing narcissism which leads to her downfall.

8. Another aspect of repressed female sexuality which finds expression in *Ghare Baire* is that of young childless widows. Forced into a life of severe abstinence and prayer, widows were often deprived of their rights to their property and abandoned in dire poverty in the holy city of Varanasi. Deepa Mehta gives powerful expression to their plight and their enforced prostitution in her Oscar-nominated film *Water*. The question of inheritance and financial support from Nikhilesh to the widows of his elder brothers and Bimola's resentment towards his generosity towards them haunts *Ghare Baire* as well. Ray uses colour contrasts to give powerful expression to a widow's life. The pallor of Bimola's sister-in-law, the stark whiteness of her unadorned widow's weeds are initially contrasted with the rich colours of the ornate interiors of the mansion, the extravagant toiletry of Bimola's dressing table. Ray's camera includes in a single frame the rather dark and plain Bimola changing her expensive and colorful velvet jackets one after another before the dressing table mirror and the reflection of the beautiful sister-in-law in the cruel, irrevocable whiteness of her saree and chemise. The sister-in-law makes an overt comment on Nikhilesh's obsessive love for his wife. She calls it an addiction and contrasts it to her own marriage which remained unconsummated due to her husband's sexual indulgence with courtesans as was customary for the *zamindars* of the time. However, the same sister-in-law has her lips reddened by the betel juice forbidden to her, a sign of her inability to accept in totality the sexual abstinence and denial that widowhood forcibly imposes upon her.[She repeatedly contrasts herself with the eldest sister-in-law committed to obligatory ritualistic worship (she worships Nandagopal, a child image of Lord Krishna, which may be interpreted as a childless widow's wish fulfillment through religious observances dedicated to a child god). She sings snatches of lyrics suggestive of extra-marital

love. She listens to lewd songs from folk theatre being emitted rather shrilly by a cranked up gramophone and gossips with her maids rather than restrict herself to the life of prayers and elaborate ritualism. Her relationship with her younger brother-in-law Nikhilesh carries sweet memories of an intimacy built up since the day she entered the gilded prison of the *zamindar's* mansion as a child bride of nine, but it is a relationship of which Bimola is instinctively jealous. Nikhilesh, at the end of the novel realises how this unfortunate woman, deprived by fate of husband and child, had nurtured this one relationship with all the stored up nectar of her heart. It brings him great solace amidst the domestic storm that ruins his life. It is one which could teeter dangerously on the sexual given the proximity of age and the shared experience of growing up together in an *andar mahal* environment which was certainly hostile for a child bride where the only sympathetic ear was that of the husband's younger brother.

9. Female sexuality and extra-marital relationships were, and continue to be a sensitive issue in Bengali films despite portrayals in later films, including Ray's own in a film like *Pikoo*. Perhaps these issues become more sensitive to the audience given the period under consideration in the two films and the crossing and re-crossing of the peripheries of the *andar mahal* and its significant social connotations, as earlier discussed in the essay. In my opinion, the development of the theme is more convincing in the texts, particularly in *Ghare Baire*. This brings us back to the question of 'confrontation' raised in the introduction. Virginia Woolf raised the bogey of a novel's complexly nuanced idea of love in the pages of a novel being reduced to a kiss on the screen.Is the kiss really clumsily executed without adequate build-up in Ray? In *Ghare Baire* he has indeed used subtly suggestive devices like the strains of a Tagore song (*Rabindrasangeet*), recurring motifs and the device of analepsis and prolepsis to match Tagore's use of the diary method of introspection (in the same novel) to develop the

effect of sexual repression on a woman and the ensuing confusion, frustration, despair and overwhelming sense of guilt on those traversing the dangerous periphery between the inner and outer chambers. Of *Charulata*, Supriya Chaudhuri in her essay, 'Space, Interiority and Affect in Charulata and Ghare Baire,' talks of the structure of strict parallels in *Nastanirh* which Ray does not attempt to reproduce, just as there is no parallel in the novella for the densely allusive literary conversation between Amal and Charu in Ray's film turning on Bankim's distinction between the traditional and contemporary woman, the *prachina* and the *nabina* which builds up a secret kinship leading up to Charu's sexual attraction for her young brother-in-law. If the response of the Western audience was not unanimously favourable, we have to remember the many contentious issues that Ray had to wrestle with in his adaptation of these texts.

Liberal Views of Osho Rajneesh, the spiritual guru and philosopher on Sexual repression and orthodoxy:

"Sex is raw energy. It has to be transformed, and through transformation there is transcendence. Rather than transforming it, religions have been repressing it. And if you repress it the natural outcome is a perverted human being. He becomes obsessed with sex.

"The people who call me 'sex guru' are obsessed with sex. I have not talked about sex more than I have talked about meditation, love, God, prayer, but nobody seems to be interested in God, love, meditation, prayer. If I say anything about sex, immediately they jump upon it.

"Out of my three hundred books only one book concerns sex, and that, too, not in its totality. The name of the book is From Sex to Superconsciousness. Just the beginning of it is concerned with sex; as you go deeper in understanding itmoves towardssuperconsciousness, towards samadhi. Now that is the book which has reached to millions of people. It is a strange phenomenon: my other books have not reached

to so many people. There is not a single Hindu, Jaina saint, mahatma in India who has not read it. It has been discussed criticized, analyzed, commented upon in every possible way. Many books have been written against it – as if that is the only book I have written!

"Why so much emphasis? People are obsessed particularly the religious people are obsessed. This label of 'sex guru' comes from religious people."

Create Meditation Out of Sex

"The more you go into meditation through sex, the less effect sex will have. Meditation will grow from it, and out of the growing meditation a new door will open and sex will wither away. It will not be a sublimation. It will be just like dry leaves falling from a tree. The tree never even knows the leaves are falling. In the same way, you will never even know that the mechanical urge for sex is going.

"Create meditation out of sex; make sex an object of meditation. Treat it as a temple and you will transcend it and be transformed. Then sex will not be there, but there will not be any suppression, any sublimation. Sex will just become irrelevant, meaningless. You have grown beyond it. It makes no sense to you now.

"It is just like a child growing up. Now toys are meaningless. He has not sublimated anything; he has not suppressed anything. He has just grown up; he has become mature. Toys are meaningless now. They are childish and now the child is no longer a child.

"In the same way, the more you meditate, the less sex will have an appeal to you. And by and by, spontaneously, without a conscious effort to sublimate sex, energy will have a new source to flow to. The same energy that has flowed through sex will now flow through meditation. And when it flows through meditation, the divine door is being opened."

Love Is Dangerous, Sex Is Not Dangerous

"People who are afraid of love are not afraid of sex. Love is dangerous; sex is not dangerous, it can be manipulated. There are now many manuals on how to do it. You can manipulate it – sex can become a technique. Love can never become a technique. If in sex you try to remain in control, then even sex will not help to reach the ultimate. It will go to a certain point and you will drop back, because somewhere it also needs a let-go.

"That's why orgasm is becoming more and more difficult. Ejaculation is not orgasm, to give birth to children is not orgasmic. Orgasm is the involvement of the total body: mind, body, soul, all together. You vibrate, your whole being vibrates, from the toes to the head. You are no longer in control; existence has taken possession of you and you don't know who you are. It is like a madness, it is like a sleep, it is like meditation, it is like death."

Love can give new soul to Sex

When two lovers are in such a deep love that love suffices and sex has simply dropped – not that it has been dropped, not that it has been suppressed, no. It has simply disappeared from your consciousness not leaving even a scar behind; then two lovers are in such total unity... Because sex divides; the very word sex comes from a root which means division. Love unites, sex divides. Sex is the root cause of division.

Conclusion:

Hence, Social Perversion has become an increasing phenomenon rather trend of youth society in this 21^{st}century, in addition to it woman who were considered to be the most deprived gender have been raising their position to a certain extent but also adds to be some major figures in the crime diary as well. Here also we could see social perversion which deviates from the regular norms of the societal living. On adition to that the on one hand the sexual crime rates are increasing at a rapid pace and liberal views on modernized outlook has been so much discussed yet somewhere we still repress an orthodoxy stereotype mentality on Gender and Sexuality which in turn leads to several more violence to the society which again enhances an essence of Perversion and deviance. Such issues need a serious revolutionary change and should be considered a major issue to be pondered upon.

References

i. Lamminpaa A. (1995) Alcohol intoxication in childhood and adolescence. Alcohol and alcoholism. National Crime Records Bureau of India.

ii. Benega V. Velayudhan A, Jain S. (2002). The Social Cost of Alcoholism, NIMHANS Journal.

iii. Block, Marvin A. (1965) Alcoholism L Its facts and phases, Oxford University Press London.

iv. Magandeep Singh (2017) The Indian Spirit : Untold Story of Drinking in India, Penguin Random House, India.

v. Das, S.K. Balakdrishanan, Vasudevan D.M. (2006), Alcohol : its Health and Social Impact in India, The National Medical Journal of India.

vi. Manor, J. (1993) Power, Poverty and Poison : Disaster and Response in an Indian City, Sage Publication, New Delhi.

vii. World Health Organization (2018) Global Status Report on Alcohol and Health, WHO, Geneva.

viii. White, H.R., Rabiner D.L. (2011), College Drinking and Drug Use, Guilford Publications, New York City. U.S.A.

ix. Rawe David, Vasonyi, Alexender ; Flannery, Denial (1995), Sex Differences in Crime : Domeans and within sex variation have similar causes ? (Journal of Research in crime and delinquency)

x. Feminism and criminology in Britain (Heidensohn, 1995).

xi. Mathews R. (2008), Prostitution, Politics and Policy, London : Routledge Cavendish.

xii. Bedi, Kiran, Nair P.M. (2008), Human Trafficking in India, Yojana (Vol-52)

xiii. Kishwar Madhu (2008) On ligelising Prostitution, Yojana (Vol. – 52)

xiv. Gilada I.S. (1999), Prostitution in India causes, extent, prevention, and Rehabilitation; Social Problems and welfare in India, New Delhi.

xv. www.nationalcrimerecordbureau.co.in

xvi. Alexander, M., Garda. L., Kanada S., Ganatra B. (2007) Correlates of pre marital relationship among unmarried youths in Pune District, Maharashtra, India.

xvii. Ahuja R. (1997), Social Problem in India, Rawat Publication, Jaipur.

xviii. Gurley Brown, H. (1962), Sex and the single girl. New York, Bernard Geis.

xix. Mehra S., Savithri R., Coutinho L., Sexual behaviour among unmarried adolescents in Delhi, India.

xx. Ahuja.R(1997), Social Poblems In India, Rawat Publication, Jaipur

About The Author

Ms.SHREYA CHATTERJEE basically belongs to Kolkata,the city of joy and had been a great contributor in the field of sociological study in several journals and magazines. In addition to this book ,she also has two books authored in her account, "Women Era" by Vedant Publication and "Perversion in contemporary india" by Swastik Publication which earned her a wide acclaim

Printed by Libri Plureos GmbH in Hamburg,
Germany